The Story of Gunnlaug the Worm-Tongue and Raven the Skald

Anonymous

Alpha Editions

This edition published in 2024

ISBN : 9789362924636

Design and Setting By
Alpha Editions
www.alphaedis.com
Email - info@alphaedis.com

As per information held with us this book is in Public Domain.
This book is a reproduction of an important historical work. Alpha Editions uses the best technology to reproduce historical work in the same manner it was first published to preserve its original nature. Any marks or number seen are left intentionally to preserve its true form.

Contents

CHAPTER I. Of Thorstein Egilson and his Kin. ....- 1 -

CHAPTER II. Of Thorsteins Dream. ....- 2 -

CHAPTER III. Of the Birth and Fostering of Helga the Fair. ....- 4 -

CHAPTER IV. Of Gunnlaug Worm-tongue and his Kin. ....- 6 -

CHAPTER V. Of Raven and his Kin. ....- 8 -

CHAPTER VI. How Helga was vowed to Gunnlaug, and of Gunnlaug's faring abroad. ....- 9 -

CHAPTER VII. Of Gunnlaug in the East and the West. ....- 13 -

CHAPTER VIII. Of Gunnlaug in Ireland. ....- 18 -

CHAPTER IX. Of the Quarrel between Gunnlaug and Raven before the Swedish King. ....- 21 -

CHAPTER X. How Raven came home to Iceland, and asked for Helga to Wife. ....- 23 -

CHAPTER XI. Of how Gunnlaug must needs abide away from Iceland. ....- 25 -

CHAPTER XII. Of Gunnlaug's landing, and how he found Helga wedded to Raven. ....- 27 -

CHAPTER XIII. Of the Winter-Wedding at Skaney, and how Gunnlaug gave the Kings Cloak to Helga. ....- 28 -

CHAPTER XIV. Of the Holmgang at the Althing. ....- 32 -

CHAPTER XV. How Gunnlaug and Raven agreed to go East to Norway, to try the matter again. ....- 35 -

CHAPTER XVI. How the two Foes met and fought at Dingness. ....- 37 -

CHAPTER XVII. The News of the Fight brought to Iceland. ....- 40 -

CHAPTER XVIII. The Death of Helga the Fair. ....- 42 -

CHAPTER I. Of Thorstein Egilson and his Kin.

There was a man called Thorstein, the son of Egil, the son of Skallagrim, the son of Kveldulf the Hersir of Norway. Asgerd was the mother of Thorstein; she was the daughter of Biorn Hold. Thorstein dwelt at Burg in Burg-firth; he was rich of fee, and a great chief, a wise man, meek and of measure in all wise. He was nought of such wondrous growth and strength as his father Egil had been; yet was he a right mighty man, and much beloved of all folk.

Thorstein was goodly to look on, flaxen-haired, and the best-eyed of men; and so say men of lore that many of the kin of the Mere-men, who are come of Egil, have been the goodliest folk; yet, for all that, this kindred have differed much herein, for it is said that some of them have been accounted the most ill-favoured of men: but in that kin have been also many men of great prowess in many wise, such as Kiartan, the son of Olaf Peacock, and Slaying-Bardi, and Skuli, the son of Thorstein. Some have been great bards, too, in that kin, as Biorn, the champion of Hit-dale, priest Einar Skulison, Snorri Sturluson, and many others.

Now, Thorstein had to wife Jofrid, the daughter of Gunnar, the son of Hlifar. This Gunnar was the best skilled in weapons, and the lithest of limb of all bonderfolk who have been in Iceland; the second was Gunnar of Lithend; but Steinthor of Ere was the third. Jofrid was eighteen winters old when Thorstein wedded her; she was a widow, for Thorodd, son of Odd of Tongue, had had her to wife aforetime. Their daughter was Hungerd, who was brought up at Thorstein's at Burg. Jofrid was a very stirring woman; she and Thorstein had many children betwixt them, but few of them come into this tale. Skuli was the eldest of their sons, Kollsvein the second, Egil the third.

CHAPTER II. Of Thorsteins Dream.

One summer, it is said, a ship came from over the main into Gufaros. Bergfinn was he hight who was the master thereof, a Northman of kin, rich in goods, and somewhat stricken in years, and a wise man he was withal.

Now, goodman Thorstein rode to the ship, as it was his wont mostly to rule the market, and this he did now. The Eastmen got housed, but Thorstein took the master to himself, for thither he prayed to go. Bergfinn was of few words throughout the winter, but Thorstein treated him well The Eastman had great joy of dreams.

One day in spring-tide Thorstein asked Bergfinn if he would ride with him up to Hawkfell, where at that time was the Thing-stead of the Burg-firthers; for Thorstein had been told that the walls of his booth had fallen in. The Eastman said he had good will to go, so that day they rode, some three together, from home, and the house-carles of Thorstein withal, till they came up under Hawkfell to a farmstead called Foxholes. There dwelt a man of small wealth called Atli, who was Thorstein's tenant Thorstein bade him come and work with them, and bring with him hoe and spade. This he did, and when they came to the tofts of the booth, they set to work all of them, and did out the walls.

The weather was hot with sunshine that day, and Thorstein and the Eastman grew heavy; and when they had moved out the walls, those two sat down within the tofts, and Thorstein slept, and fared ill in his sleep. The Eastman sat beside him, and let him have his dream fully out, and when he awoke he was much wearied. Then the Eastman asked him what he had dreamt, as he had had such an ill time of it in his sleep.

Thorstein said, "Nay, dreams betoken nought."

But as they rode homeward in the evening, the Eastman asked him again what he had dreamt.

Thorstein said, "If I tell thee the dream, then shalt thou unriddle it to me, as it verily is."

The Eastman said he would risk it.

Then Thorstein said: "This was my dream; for methought I was at home at Burg, standing outside the men's-door, and I looked up at the house-roof, and on the ridge I saw a swan, goodly and fair, and I thought it was mine own, and deemed it good beyond all things. Then I saw a great eagle sweep down from the mountains, and fly thitherward and alight beside the swan, and chuckle over her lovingly; and methouht the swan seemed well content therewith; but I noted that the eagle was black-eyed, and that on him were iron claws: valiant he seemed to me.

"After this I thought I saw another fowl come flying from the south quarter, and he, too, came hither to Burg, and sat down on the house beside the swan, and would fain be fond with her. This also was a mighty eagle.

"But soon I thought that the eagle first-come ruffled up at the coming of the other. Then they fought fiercely and long, and this I saw that both bled, and such was the end of their play, that each tumbled either way down from the house-roof, and there they lay both dead.

"But the swan sat left alone, drooping much, and sad of semblance.

"Then I saw a fowl fly from the west; that was a falcon, and he sat beside the swan and made fondly towards her, and they flew away both together into one and the same quarter, and therewith I awoke.

"But a dream of no mark this is," he says, "and will in all likelihood betoken gales, that they shall meet in the air from those quarters whence I deemed the fowl flew."

The Eastman spake: "I deem it nowise such," saith he.

Thorstein said, "Make of the dream, then, what seemeth likest to thee, and let me hear."

Then said the Eastman: "These birds are like to be fetches of men: but thy wife sickens now, and she will give birth to a woman-child fair and lovely; and dearly thou wilt love her; but high-born men shall woo thy daughter, coming from such quarters as the eagles seemed to fly from, and shall love her with overweening love, and shall fight about her, and both lose their lives thereby. And thereafter a third man, from the quarter whence came the falcon, shall woo her, and to that man shall she be wedded. Now, I have unravelled thy dream, and I think things will befall as I have said."

Thorstein answered: "In evil and unfriendly wise is the dream interpreted, nor do I deem thee fit for the work of unriddling dreams."

Then Eastman said, "Thou shalt find how it will come to pass."

But Thorstein estranged himself from the Eastman thenceforward, and he left that summer, and now he is out of the tale.

CHAPTER III.
Of the Birth and Fostering of Helga the Fair.

This summer Thorstein got ready to ride to the Thing, and spake to Jofrid his wife before he went from home. "So is it," he says, "that thou art with child now, but thy child shall be cast forth if thou bear a woman; but nourished if it be a man."

Now, at this time when all the land was heathen, it was somewhat the wont of such men as had little wealth, and were like to have many young children on their hands, to have them cast forth, but an evil deed it was always deemed to be.

And now, when Thorstein had said this, Jofrid answers, "This is a word all unlike thee, such a man as thou art, and surely to a wealthy man like thee it will not seem good that this should be done."

Thorstein answered: "Thou knowest my mind, and that no good will hap if my will be thwarted."

So he rode to the Thing; but while he was gone Jofrid gave birth to a woman-child wondrous fair. The women would fain show her to the mother; she said there was little need thereof, but had her shepherd Thorvard called to her, and spake to him:—

"Thou shalt take my horse and saddle it, and bring this child west to Herdholt, to Thorgerd, Egil's daughter, and pray her to nourish it secretly, so that Thorstein may not know thereof. For with such looks of love do I behold this child, that surely I cannot bear to have it cast forth. Here are three marks of silver, have them in reward of thy work; but west there Thorgerd will get thee fare and food over the sea."

Then Thorvard did her bidding; he rode with the child to Herdholt, and gave it into Thorgerd's hands, and she had it nourished at a tenant's of hers who dwelt at Freedmans-stead up in Hvamfirth; but she got fare for Thorvard north in Steingrims-firth, in Shell-creek, and gave him meet outfit for his sea-faring: he went thence abroad, and is now out of the story.

Now when Thorstein came home from the Thing, Jofrid told him that the child had been cast forth according to his word, but that the herdsman had fled away and stolen her horse. Thorstein said she had done well, and got himself another herdsman. So six winters passed, and this matter was nowise wotted of.

Now in those days Thorstein rode to Herdholt, being bidden there as guest of his brother-in-law, Olaf Peacock, the son of Hoskuld, who was then deemed to be the chief highest of worth among all men west there. Good cheer was made Thorstein, as was like to be; and one day at the feast it is said that Thorgerd sat in the high seat talking with her brother Thorstein, while Olaf was talking to other men; but on the bench right over against them sat three little maidens. Then said Thorgerd,—

"How dost thou, brother, like the look of these three little maidens sitting straight before us?"

"Right well," he answers, "but one is by far the fairest; she has all the goodliness of Olaf, but the whiteness and the countenance of us, the Mere-men."

Thorgerd answered: "Surely this is true, brother, wherein thou sayest that she has the fairness and countenance of us Mere-folk, but the goodliness of Olaf Peacock she has not got, for she is not his daughter."

"How can that be," says Thorstein, "being thy daughter none the less?"

She answered: "To say sooth, kinsman," quoth she, "this fair maiden is not my daughter, but thine."

And therewith she told him all as it had befallen, and prayed him to forgive her and his own wife that trespass.

Thorstein said: "I cannot blame you two for having done this; most things will fall as they are fated, and well have ye covered over my folly: so look I on this maiden that I deem it great good luck to have so fair a child. But now, what is her name?"

"Helga she is called," says Thorgerd.

"Helga the Fair," says Thorstein. "But now shalt thou make her ready to come home with me."

She did so, and Thorstein was led out with good gifts, and Helga rode with him to his home, and was brought up there with much honour and great love from father and mother and all her kin.

CHAPTER IV.
Of Gunnlaug Worm-tongue and his Kin.

Now at this time there dwelt at Gilsbank, up in White-water-side, Illugi the Black, son of Hallkel, the son of Hrosskel. The mother of Illugi was Thurid Dandle, daughter of Gunnlaug Worm-tongue.

Illugi was the next greatest chief in Burg-firth after Thorstein Egilson. He was a man of broad lands and hardy of mood, and wont to do well to his friends; he had to wife Ingibiorg, the daughter of Asbiorn Hordson, from Ornolfsdale; the mother of Ingibiorg was Thorgerd, the daughter of Midfirth-Skeggi. The children of Illugi and Ingibiorg were many, but few of them have to do with this story. Hermund was one of their sons, and Gunnlaug another; both were hopeful men, and at this time of ripe growth.

It is told of Gunnlaug that he was quick of growth in his early youth, big, and strong; his hair was light red, and very goodly of fashion; he was dark-eyed, somewhat ugly-nosed, yet of lovesome countenance; thin of flank he was, and broad of shoulder, and the best-wrought of men; his whole mind was very masterful; eager was he from his youth up, and in all wise unsparing and hardy; he was a great skald, but somewhat bitter in his rhyming, and therefore was he called Gunnlaug Worm-tongue.

Hermund was the best beloved of the two brothers, and had the mien of a great man.

When Gunnlaug was fifteen winters old he prayed his father for goods to fare abroad withal, and said he had will to travel and see the manners of other folk. Master Illugi was slow to take the matter up, and said he was unlike to be deemed good in the out-lands "when I can scarcely shape thee to my own liking at home."

On a morning but a very little afterwards it happened that Illugi came out early, and saw that his storehouse was opened, and that some sacks of wares, six of them, had been brought out into the road, and therewithal too some pack-gear. Now, as he wondered at this, there came up a man leading four horses, and who should it be but his son Gunnlaug. Then said he:—

"I it was who brought out the sacks."

Illugi asked him why he had done so. He said that they should make his faring goods.

Illugi said: "In nowise shalt thou thwart my will, nor fare anywhere sooner than I like!" and in again he swung the ware-sacks therewith.

Then Gunnlaug rode thence and came in the evening down to Burg, and goodman Thorstein asked him to bide there, and Gunnlaug was fain of that proffer. He told Thorstein how things had gone betwixt him and his father, and Thorstein offered to let him bide there as long as he liked, and for some seasons Gunnlaug abode there, and learned law-craft of Thorstein, and all men accounted well of him.

Now Gunnlaug and Helga would be always at the chess-playing together, and very soon each found favour with the other, as came to be proven well enough afterwards: they were very nigh of an age.

Helga was so fair, that men of lore say that she was the fairest woman of Iceland, then or since; her hair was so plenteous and long that it could cover her all over, and it was as fair as a band of gold; nor was there any so good to choose as Helga the Fair in all Burgfirth, and far and wide elsewhere.

Now one day, as men sat in the hall at Burg, Gunnlaug spake to Thorstein: "One thing in law there is which thou hast not taught me, and that is how to woo me a wife."

Thorstein said, "That is but a small matter," and therewith taught him how to go about it.

Then said Gunnlaug, "Now shalt thou try if I have understood all: I shall take thee by the hand and make as if I were wooing thy daughter Helga."

"I see no need of that," says Thorstein. Gunnlaug, however, groped then and there after his hand, and seizing it said, "Nay, grant me this though."

"Do as thou wilt, then," said Thorstein; "but be it known to all who are hereby that this shall be as if it had been unspoken, nor shall any guile follow herein."

Then Gunnlaug named for himself witnesses, and betrothed Helga to him, and asked thereafter if it would stand good thus. Thorstein said that it was well; and those who were present were mightily pleased at all this.

CHAPTER V. Of Raven and his Kin.

There was a man called Onund, who dwelt in the south at Mossfell: he was the wealthiest of men, and had a priesthood south there about the nesses. He was married, and his wife was called Geirny. She was the daughter of Gnup, son of Mold-Gnup, who settled at Grindwick, in the south country. Their sons were Raven, and Thorarin, and Eindridi; they were all hopeful men, but Raven was in all wise the first of them. He was a big man and a strong, the sightliest of men and a good skald; and when he was fully grown he fared between sundry lands, and was well accounted of wherever he came.

Thorod the Sage, the son of Eyvind, then dwelt at Hjalli, south in Olfus, with Skapti his son, who was then the spokesman-at-law in Iceland. The mother of Skapti was Ranveig, daughter of Gnup, the son of Mold-Gnup; and Skapti and the sons of Onund were sisters' sons. Between these kinsmen was much friendship as well as kinship.

At this time Thorfin, the son of Selthorir, dwelt at Red-Mel, and had seven sons, who were all the hopefullest of men; and of them were these—Thorgils, Eyjolf, and Thorir; and they were all the greatest men out there. But these men who have now been named lived all at one and the same time.

Next to this befell those tidings, the best that ever have befallen here in Iceland, that the whole land became Christian, and that all folk cast off the old faith.

CHAPTER VI.
How Helga was vowed to Gunnlaug, and of Gunnlaug's faring abroad.

Gunnlaug Worm-Tongue was, as is aforesaid, whiles at Burg with Thorstein, whiles with his father Illugi at Gilsbank, three winters together, and was by now eighteen winters old; and father and son were now much more of a mind.

There was a man called Thorkel the Black; he was a house-carle of Illugi, and near akin to him, and had been brought up in his house. To him fell an heritage north at As, in Water-dale, and he prayed Gunnlaug to go with him thither. This he did, and so they rode, the two together, to As. There they got the fee; it was given up to them by those who had the keeping of it, mostly because of Gunnlaug's furtherance.

But as they rode from the north they guested at Grimstongue, at a rich bonder's who dwelt there; but in the morning a herdsman took Gunnlaug's horse, and it had sweated much by then he got it back. Then Gunnlaug smote the herdsman, and stunned him; but the bonder would in nowise bear this, and claimed boot therefor. Gunnlaug offered to pay him one mark. The bonder thought it too little.

Then Gunnlaug sang,—

> *"Bade I the middling mighty*
> *To have a mark of waves' flame;*
> *Giver of grey seas? glitter,*
> *This gift shalt thou make shift with.*
> *If the elf sun of the waters*
> *From out of purse thou lettest,*
> *O waster of the worm's bedy*
> *Awaits thee sorrow later."*

So the peace was made as Gunnlaug bade, and in such wise the two rode south.

Now, a little while after, Gunnlaug asked his father a second time for goods for going abroad.

Illugi says, "Now shalt thou have thy will, for thou hast wrought thyself into something better than thou wert." So Illugi rode hastily from home, and bought for Gunnlaug half a ship which lay in Gufaros, from Audun Festargram—this Audun was he who would not flit abroad the sons of Oswif the Wise, after the slaying of Kiartan Olafson, as is told in the story of the Laxdalemen, which thing though betid later than this.—And when Illugi came home, Gunnlaug thanked him well.

Thorkel the Black betook himself to seafaring with Gunnlaug, and their wares were brought to the ship; but Gunnlaug was at Burg while they made her ready, and found more cheer in talk with Helga than in toiling with chapmen.

Now one day Thorstein asked Gunnlaug if he would ride to his horses with him up to Long-water-dale. Gunnlaug said he would. So they ride both together till they come to the mountain-dairies of Thorstein, called Thorgils-stead. There were stud-horses of Thorstein, four of them together, all red of hue. There was one horse very goodly, but little tried: this horse Thorstein offered to give to Gunnlaug. He said he was in no need of horses, as he was going away from the country; and so they ride to other stud-horses. There was a grey horse with four mares, and he was the best of horses in Burgfirth. This one, too, Thorstein offered to give Gunnlaug, but he said, "I desire these in no wise more than the others; but why dost thou not bid me what I will take?"

"What is that?" said Thorstein.

"Helga the Fair, thy daughter," says Gunnlaug.

"That rede is not to be settled so hastily," said Thorstein; and therewithal got on other talk. And now they ride homewards down along Long-water.

Then said Gunnlaug, "I must needs know what thou wilt answer me about the wooing."

Thorstein answers: "I heed not thy vain talk," says he.

Gunnlaug says, "This is my whole mind, and no vain words."

Thorstein says, "Thou shouldst first know thine own will. Art thou not bound to fare abroad? and yet thou makest as if thou wouldst go marry. Neither art thou an even match for Helga while thou art so unsettled, and therefore this cannot so much as be looked at."

Gunnlaug says, "Where lookest thou for a match for thy daughter, if thou wilt not give her to the son of Illugi the Black; or who are they throughout Burg-firth who are of more note than he?"

Thorstein answered: "I will not play at men-mating," says he, "but if thou wert such a man as he is, thou wouldst not be turned away."

Gunnlaug said, "To whom wilt thou give thy daughter rather than to me?"

Said Thorstein, "Hereabout are many good men to choose from. Thorfin of Red-Mel hath seven sons, and all of them men of good manners."

Gunnlaug answers, "Neither Onund nor Thorfin are men as good as my father. Nay, thou thyself clearly fallest short of him—or what hast thou to set against his strife with Thorgrim the Priest, the son of Kiallak, and his sons, at Thorsness Thing, where he carried all that was in debate?"

Thorstein answers, "I drave away Steinar, the son of Onund Sioni, which was deemed somewhat of a deed."

Gunnlaug says, "Therein thou wast holpen by thy father Egil; and, to end all, it is for few bonders to cast away my alliance."

Said Thorstein, "Carry thy cowing away to the fellows up yonder at the mountains; for down here, on the Meres, it shall avail thee nought."

Now in the evening they come home; but next morning Gunnlaug rode up to Gilsbank, and prayed his father to ride with him a-wooing out to Burg.

Illugi answered, "Thou art an unsettled man, being bound for faring abroad, but makest now as if thou wouldst busy thyself with wife-wooing; and so much do I know, that this is not to Thorstein's mind."

Gunnlaug answers, "I shall go abroad all the same, nor shall I be well pleased but if thou further this."

So after this Illugi rode with eleven men from home down to Burg, and Thorstein greeted him well. Early in the morning Illugi said to Thorstein, "I would speak to thee."

"Let us go, then, to the top of the Burg, and talk together there," says Thorstein; and so they did, and Gunnlaug went with them.

Then said Illugi, "My kinsman Gunnlaug tells me that he has begun a talk with thee on his own behalf, praying that he might woo thy daughter Helga; but now I would fain know what is like to come of this matter. His kin is known to thee, and our possessions; from my hand shall be spared neither land nor rule over men, if such things might perchance further matters."

Thorstein said, "Herein alone Gunnlaug pleases me not, that I find him an unsettled man; but if he were of a mind like thine, little would I hang back."

Illugi said, "It will cut our friendship across if thou gainsayest me and my son an equal match."

Thorstein answers, "For thy words and our friendship then, Helga shall be vowed, but not betrothed, to Gunnlaug, and shall bide for him three winters: but Gunnlaug shall go abroad and shape himself to the ways of good men; but I shall be free from all these matters if he does not then come back, or if his ways are not to my liking."

Thereat they parted; Illugi rode home, but Gunnlaug rode to his ship. But when they had wind at will they sailed for the main, and made the northern part of Norway, and sailed landward along Thrandheim to Nidaros; there they rode in the harbour, and unshipped their goods.

CHAPTER VII. Of Gunnlaug in the East and the West.

In those days Earl Eric, the son of Hakon, and his brother Svein, ruled in Norway. Earl Eric abode as then at Hladir, which was left to him by his father, and a mighty lord he was. Skuli, the son of Thorstein, was with the earl at that time, and was one of his court, and well esteemed.

Now they say that Gunnlaug and Audun Festargram, and seven of them together, went up to Hladir to the earl. Gunnlaug was so clad that he had on a grey kirtle and white long-hose; he had a boil on his foot by the instep, and from this oozed blood and matter as he strode on. In this guise he went before the earl with Audun and the rest of them, and greeted him well. The earl knew Audun, and asked him tidings from Iceland. Audun told him what there was toward. Then the earl asked Gunnlaug who he was, and Gunnlaug told him his name and kin. Then the earl said: "Skuli Thorstein's son, what manner of man is this in Iceland?"

"Lord," says he, "give him good welcome, for he is the son of the best man in Iceland, Illugi the Black of Gilsbank, and my foster-brother withal."

The earl asked, "What ails thy foot, Icelander?"

"A boil, lord," said he.

"And yet thou wentest not halt?"

Gunnlaug answers, "Why go halt while both legs are long alike?"

Then said one of the earl's men, called Thorir: "He swaggereth hugely, this Icelander! It would not be amiss to try him a little."

Gunnlaug looked at him and sang:—

> "A courtman there is
> Full evil I wis,
> A bad man and black,
> Belief let him lack."

Then would Thorir seize an axe. The earl spake: "Let it be," says he; "to such things men should pay no heed. But now, Icelander, how old a man art thou?"

Gunnlaug answers: "I am eighteen winters old as now," says he.

Then says Earl Eric, "My spell is that thou shalt not live eighteen winters more."

Gunnlaug said, somewhat under his breath: "Pray not against me, but for thyself rather."

The earl asked thereat, "What didst thou say, Icelander?"

Gunnlaug answers, "What I thought well befitting, that thou shouldst bid no prayers against me, but pray well for thyself rather."

"What prayers, then?" says the earl.

"That thou mightest not meet thy death after the manner of Earl Hakon, thy father."

The earl turned red as blood, and bade them take the rascal in haste; but Skuli stepped up to the earl, and said: "Do this for my words, lord, and give this man peace, so that he depart at his swiftest."

The earl answered, "At his swiftest let him be off then, if he will have peace, and never let him come again within my realm."

Then Skuli went out with Gunnlaug down to the bridges, where there was an England-bound ship ready to put out; therein Skuli got for Gunnlaug a berth, as well as for Thorkel, his kinsman; but Gunnlaug gave his ship into Audun's ward, and so much of his goods as he did not take with him.

Now sail Gunnlaug and his fellows into the English main, and come at autumntide south to London Bridge, where they hauled ashore their ship.

Now at that time King Ethelred, the son of Edgar, ruled over England, and was a good lord; this winter he sat in London. But in those days there was the same tongue in England as in Norway and Denmark; but the tongues changed when William the Bastard won England, for thenceforward French went current there, for he was of French kin.

Gunnlaug went presently to the king, and greeted him well and worthily, The king asked him from what land he came, and Gunnlaug told him all as it was. "But," said he, "I have come to meet thee, lord, for that I have made a song on thee, and I would that it might please thee to hearken to that song." The king said it should be so, and Gunnlaug gave forth the song well and proudly; and this is the burden thereof:—

"As God are all folk fearing

The free lord King of England,

> *Kin of all kings and all folk,*
>
> *To Ethelred the head tow."*

The king thanked him for the song, and gave him as song-reward a scarlet cloak lined with the costliest of furs, and golden-broidered down to the hem; and made him his man; and Gunnlaug was with him all the winter, and was well accounted of.

One day, in the morning early, Gunnlaug met three men in a certain street, and Thrororm was the name of their leader; he was big and strong, and right evil to deal with. He said, "Northman, lend me some money."

Gunnlaug answered, "That were ill counselled to lend one's money to unknown men."

He said, "I will pay it thee back on a named day."

"Then shall it be risked," says Gunnlaug; and he lent him the fee withal.

But some time afterwards Gunnlaug met the king, and told him of the money-lending. The king answered, "Now hast thou thriven little, for this is the greatest robber and reiver; deal with him in no wise, but I will give thee money as much as thine was."

Gunnlaug said, "Then do we, your men, do after a sorry sort, if, treading sackless folk under foot, we let such fellows as this deal us out our lot. Nay, that shall never be."

Soon after he met Thrororm and claimed the fee of him. He said he was not going to pay it.

Then sang Gunnlaug:—

> *"Evil counselled art thou,*
>
> *Gold from us withholding;*
>
> *The reddener of the edges,*
>
> *Pricking on with tricking.*
>
> *Wot ye what? they called me,*
>
> *Worm-tongue, yet a youngling;*
>
> *Nor for nought so hight I;*
>
> *Now is time to show it!"*

"Now I will make an offer good in law," says Gunnlaug; "that thou either pay me my money, or else that thou go on holm with me in three nights' space."

Then laughed the viking, and said, "Before thee none have come to that, to call me to holm, despite of all the ruin that many a man has had to take at my hands. Well, I am ready to go."

Thereon they parted for that time.

Gunnlaug told the king what had befallen; and he said, "Now, indeed, have things taken a right hopeless turn; for this man's eyes can dull any weapon. But thou shalt follow my rede; here is a sword I will give thee—with that thou shalt fight, but before the battle show him another."

Gunnlaug thanked the king well therefor.

Now when they were ready for the holm, Thororm asked what sort of a sword it was that he had. Gunnlaug unsheathed it and showed him, but had a loop round the handle of the king's sword, and slipped it over his hand; the bearserk looked on the sword, and said, "I fear not that sword."

But now he dealt a blow on Gunnlaug with his sword, and cut off from him nigh all his shield; Gunnlaug smote in turn with the king's gift; the bearserk stood shieldless before him, thinking he had the same weapon he had shown him, but Gunnlaug smote him his deathblow then and there.

The king thanked him for this work, and he got much fame therefor, both in England and far and wide elsewhere.

In the spring, when ships sailed from land to land, Gunnlaug prayed King Ethelred for leave to sail somewhither; the king asks what he was about then. Gunnlaug said, "I would fulfil what I have given my word to do," and sang this stave withal:—

> *"My ways must I be wending*
>
> *Three kings' walls to see yet,*
>
> *And earls twain, as I promised*
>
> *Erewhile to land-sharers.*
>
> *Neither will I wend me*

> *Back, the worms'-bed lacking,*
> *By war-lord's son, the wealth-free,*
> *For work done gift well given."*

"So be it, then, skald," said the king, and withal he gave him a ring that weighed six ounces; "but," said he, "thou shalt give me thy word to come back next autumn, for I will not let thee go altogether, because of thy great prowess."

CHAPTER VIII. Of Gunnlaug in Ireland.

Thereafter Gunnlaug sailed from England with chapmen north to Dublin. In those days King Sigtrygg Silky-beard, son of King Olaf Kvaran and Queen Kormlada, ruled over Ireland; and he had then borne sway but a little while. Gunnlaug went before the king, and greeted him well and worthily. The king received him as was meet. Then Gunnlaug said, "I have made a song on thee, and I would fain have silence therefor."

The king answered, "No men have before now come forward with songs for me, and surely will I hearken to thine." Then Gunnlaug brought the song, whereof this is the burden,—

"Swaru's steed

Doth Sigtrygg feed."

And this is therein also:—

"Praise-worth I can

Well measure in man,

And kings, one by one—

Lo here, Kvararis son!

Grualgeth the king

Gift of gold ring?

I, singer, know

His wont to bestow.

Let the high king say,

Heard he or this day,

Song drapu-measure

Dearer a treasure?"

The king thanked him for the song, and called his treasurer to him, and said, "How shall the song be rewarded?"

"What hast thou will to give, lord?" says he.

"How will it be rewarded if I give him two ships for it?" said the king.

Then said the treasurer, "This is too much, lord; other kings give in regard of songs good keepsakes, fair swords, or golden rings."

So the king gave him his own raiment of new scarlet, a gold-embroidered kirtle, and a cloak lined with choice furs, and a gold ring which weighed a mark. Gunnlaug thanked him well.

He dwelt a short time here, and then went thence to the Orkneys.

Then was lord in Orkney, Earl Sigurd, the son of Hlodver; he was friendly to Icelanders. Now Gunnlaug greeted the earl well, and said he had a song to bring him. The earl said he would listen thereto, since he was of such great kin in Iceland.

Then Gunnlaug brought the song; it was a shorter lay, and well done. The earl gave him for lay-reward a broad axe, all inlaid with silver, and bade him abide with him.

Gunnlaug thanked him both for his gift and his offer, but said he was bound east for Sweden; and thereafter he went on board ship with chapmen who sailed to Norway.

In the autumn they came east to King's Cliff, Thorkel, his kinsman, being with him all the time. From King's Cliff they got a guide up to West Gothland, and came upon a cheaping-stead, called Skarir: there ruled an earl called Sigurd, a man stricken in years. Gunnlaug went before him, and told him he had made a song on him; the earl gave a willing ear hereto, and Gunnlaug brought the song, which was a shorter lay.

The earl thanked him, and rewarded the song well, and bade him abide there that winter.

Earl Sigurd had a great Yule-feast in the winter, and on Yule-eve came thither men sent from Earl Eric of Norway, twelve of them together, and brought gifts to Earl Sigurd. The earl made them good cheer, and bade them sit by Gunnlaug through the Yule-tide; and there was great mirth at drinks.

Now the Gothlanders said that no earl was greater or of more fame than Earl Sigurd; but the Norwegians thought that Earl Eric was by far the foremost of the two. Hereon would they bandy words, till they both took Gunnlaug to be umpire in the matter.

Then he sang this stave:—

"Tell ye, staves of spear-din,

How on sleek-side sea-horse

> *Oft this earl hath proven*
> *Over-toppling billows;*
> *But Eric, victory's ash-tree,*
> *Oft hath seen in east-seas*
> *More of high blue billows*
> *Before the bows a-roaring."*

Both sides were content with his finding, but the Norwegians the best. But after Yule-tide those messengers left with gifts of goodly things, which Earl Sigurd sent to Earl Eric.

Now they told Earl Eric of Gunnlaug's finding: the earl thought that he had shown upright dealing and friendship to him herein, and let out some words, saying that Gunnlaug should have good peace throughout his land. What the earl had said came thereafter to the ears of Gunnlaug.

But now Earl Sigurd gave Gunnlaug a guide east to Tenthland, in Sweden, as he had asked.

CHAPTER IX.
Of the Quarrel between Gunnlaug and Raven before the Swedish King.

In those days King Ola the Swede, son of King Eric the Victorious, and Sigrid the High-counselled, daughter of Skogul Tosti, ruled over Sweden. He was a mighty king and renowned, and full fain of fame.

Gunnlaug came to Upsala towards the time of the Thing of the Swedes in spring-tide; and when he got to see the king, he greeted him. The king took his greeting well, and asked who he was. He said he was an Iceland-man.

Then the king called out: "Raven," says he, "what man is he in Iceland?"

Then one stood up from the lower bench, a big man and a stalwart, and stepped up before the king, and spake: "Lord," says he, "he is of good kin, and himself the most stalwart of men."

"Let him go, then, and sit beside thee," said the king.

Then Gunnlaug said, "I have a song to set forth before thee, king, and I would fain have peace while thou hearkenest thereto."

"Go ye first, and sit ye down," says the king, "for there is no leisure now to sit listening to songs."

So they did as he bade them.

Now Gunnlaug and Raven fell a-talking together, and each told each of his travels. Raven said that he had gone the summer before from Iceland to Norway, and had come east to Sweden in the forepart of winter. They soon got friendly together.

But one day, when the Thing was over, they were both before the king, Gunnlaug and Raven.

Then spake Gunnlaug, "Now, lord, I would that thou shouldst hear the song."

"That I may do now," said the king.

"My song too will I set forth now," says Raven.

"Thou mayst do so," said the king.

Then Gunnlaug said, "I will set forth mine first if thou wilt have it so, king."

"Nay," said Raven, "it behoveth me to be first, lord, for I myself came first to thee."

"Whereto came our fathers forth, so that my father was the little boat towed behind? Whereto, but nowhere?" says Gunnlaug. "And in likewise shall it be with us."

Raven answered, "Let us be courteous enough not to make this a matter of bandying of words. Let the king rule here."

The king said, "Let Gunnlaug set forth his song first, for he will not be at peace till he has his will."

Then Gunnlaug set forth the song which he had made to King Olaf, and when it was at an end the king spake. "Raven," says he, "how is the song done?"

"Right well," he answered; "it is a song full of big words and little beauty; a somewhat rugged song, as is Gunnlaug's own mood."

"Well, Raven, thy song," said the king.

Raven gave it forth, and when it was done the king said, "How is this song made, Gunnlaug?"

"Well it is, lord," he said; "this is a pretty song, as is Raven himself to behold, and delicate of countenance. But why didst thou make a short song on the king, Raven? Didst thou perchance deem him unworthy of a long one?"

Raven answered, "Let us not talk longer on this; matters will be taken up again, though it be later."

And thereat, they parted.

Soon after Raven became a man of King Olaf's, and asked him leave to go away. This the king granted him. And when Raven was ready to go, he spake to Gunnlaug, and said, "Now shall our friendship be ended, for that thou must needs shame me here before great men; but in time to come I shall cast on thee no less shame than thou hadst will to cast on me here."

Gunnlaug answers: "Thy threats grieve me nought. Nowhere are we likely to come where I shall be thought less worthy than thou."

King Olaf gave to Raven good gifts at parting, and thereafter.

CHAPTER X.
How Raven came home to Iceland, and asked for Helga to Wife.

Now this spring Raven came from the east to Thrandheim, and fitted out his ship, and sailed in the summer to Iceland. He brought his ship to Leiruvag, below the Heath, and his friends and kinsmen were right fain of him. That winter he was at home with his father, but the summer after he met at the Althing his kinsman, Skapti the law-man.

Then said Raven to him, "Thine aid would I have to go a-wooing to Thorstein Egilson, to bid Helga his daughter."

Skapti answered, "But is she not already vowed to Gunnlaug Worm-tongue?"

Said Raven, "Is not the appointed time of waiting between them passed by? And far too wanton is he withal, that he should hold or heed it aught."

"Let us then do as thou wouldst," said Skapti.

Thereafter they went with many men to the booth of Thorstein Egilson, and he greeted them well.

Then Skapti spoke: "Raven, my kinsman, is minded to woo thy daughter Helga. Thou knowest well his blood, his wealth, and his good manners, his many mighty kinsmen and friends."

Thorstein said, "She is already the vowed maiden of Gunnlaug, and with him shall I hold all words spoken."

Skapti said, "Are not the three winters worn now that were named between you?"

"Yes," said Thorstein; "but the summer is not yet worn, and he may still come out this summer."

Then Skapti said, "But if he cometh not this summer, what hope may we have of the matter then?"

Thorstein answered, "We are like to come here next summer, and then may we see what may wisely be done, but it will not do to speak hereof longer as at this time."

Thereon they parted. And men rode home from the Althing. But this talk of Raven's wooing of Helga was nought hidden.

That summer Gunnlaug came not out.

The next summer, at the Althing, Skapti and his folk pushed the wooing eagerly, and said that Thorstein was free as to all matters with Gunnlaug.

Thorstein answered, "I have few daughters to see to, and fain am I that they should not be the cause of strife to any man. Now I will first see Illugi the Black." And so he did. .

And when they met, he said to Illugi, "Dost thou not think that I am free from all troth with thy son Gunnlaug?"

Illugi said, "Surely, if thou wiliest it. Little can I say herein, as I do not know clearly what Gunnlaug is about."

Then Thorstein went to Skapti, and a bargain was struck that the wedding should be at Burg, about winter-nights, if Gunnlaug did not come out that summer; but that Thorstein should be free from all troth with Raven if Gunnlaug should come and fetch his bride.

After this men ride home from the Thing, and Gunnlaug's coming was long drawn out. But Helga thought evilly of all these redes.

CHAPTER XI.
Of how Gunnlaug must needs abide away from Iceland.

Now it is to be told of Gunnlaug that he went from Sweden the same summer that Raven went to Iceland, and good gifts he had from King Olaf at parting.

King Ethelred welcomed Gunnlaug worthily, and that winter he was with the king, and was held in great honour.

In those days Knut the Great, son of Svein, ruled Denmark, and had new-taken his father's heritage, and he vowed ever to wage war on England, for that his father had won a great realm there before he died west in that same land.

And at that time there was a great army of Danish men west there, whose chief was Heming, the son of Earl Strut-Harald, and brother to Earl Sigvaldi, and he held for King Knut that land that Svein had won.

Now in the spring Gunnlaug asked the king for leave to go away, but he said, "It ill beseems that thou, my man, shouldst go away now, when all bodes such mighty war in the land."

Gunnlaug said, "Thou shalt rule, lord; but give me leave next summer to depart, if the Danes come not."

The king answered, "Then we shall see."

Now this summer went by, and the next winter, but no Danes came; and after midsummer Gunnlaug got his leave to depart from the king, and went thence east to Norway, and found Earl Eric in Thrandheim, at Hladir, and the earl greeted him well, and bade him abide with him. Gunnlaug thanked him for his offer, but said he would first go out to Iceland, to look to his promised maiden.

The earl said, "Now all ships bound for Iceland have sailed."

Then said one of the court, "Here lay, yesterday, Hallfred Troublous-Skald, out tinder Agdaness."

The earl answered, "That may well be; he sailed hence five nights ago."

Then Earl Eric had Gunnlaug rowed put to Hallfred, who greeted him with joy; and forthwith a fair wind bore them from land, and they were right merry.

This was late in the summer: but now Hallfred said to Gunnlaug, "Hast thou heard of how Raven, the son of Onund, is wooing Helga the Fair?"

Gunnlaug said he had heard thereof but dimly. Hallfred tells him all he knew of it, and therewith, too, that it was the talk of many men that Raven was in nowise less brave a man than Gunnlaug. Then Gunnlaug sang this stave:—

> *"Light the weather wafteth;*
>
> *But if this east wind drifted*
>
> *Week-long, wild upon us*
>
> *Little were I recking;*
>
> *More this word I mind of*
>
> *Me with Raven mated,*
>
> *Than gain for me the gold-foe*
>
> *Of days to make me grey-haired."*

Then Hallfred said, "Well, fellow, may'st thou fare better in thy strife with Raven than I did in mine. I brought my ship some winters ago into Leiruvag, and had to pay a half-mark in silver to a house-carle of Raven's, but I held it back from him. So Raven rode at us with sixty men, and cut the moorings of the ship, and she was driven up on the shallows, and we were bound for a wreck. Then I had to give selfdoom to Raven, and a whole mark I had to pay; and that is the tale of my dealings with him."

Then they two talked together alone of Helga the Fair, and Gunnlaug praised her much for her goodliness; and Gunnlaug sang:—

> *"He who brand of battle*
>
> *Beareth over-wary,*
>
> *Never love shall let him*
>
> *Hold the linen-folded;*
>
> *For we when we were younger*
>
> *In many a way were playing*
>
> *On the outward nesses*
>
> *From golden land outstanding."*

"Well sung!" said Hallfred.

CHAPTER XII.
Of Gunnlaug's landing, and how he found Helga wedded to Raven.

They made land north by Fox-Plain, in Hraunhaven, half a month before winter, and there unshipped their goods. Now there was a man called Thord, a bonder's son of the Plain, there. He fell to wrestling with the chapmen, and they mostly got worsted at his hands.

Then a wrestling was settled between him and Gunnlaug. The night before Thord made vows to Thor for the victory; but the next day, when they met, they fell-to wrestling. Then Gunnlaug tripped both feet from under Thord, and gave him a. great fall; but the foot that Gunnlaug stood on was put out of joint, and Gunnlaug fell together with Thord.

Then said Thord, "Maybe that other things go no better for thee."

"What then?" says Gunnlaug.

"Thy dealings with Raven, if he wed Helga the Fair at winter-nights. I was anigh at the Thing when that was settled last summer."

Gunnlaug answered naught thereto.

Now the foot was swathed, and put into joint again, and it swelled mightily; but he and Hallfred ride twelve in company till they come to Gilsbank, in Burg-firth, the very Saturday night when folk sat at the wedding at Burg. Illugi was fain of his son Gunnlaug and his fellows; but Gunnlaug said he would ride then and there down to Burg. Illugi said it was not wise to do so, and to all but Gunnlaug that seemed good. But Gunnlaug was then unfit to walk, because of his foot, though he would not let that be seen. Therefore there was no faring to Burg.

On the morrow Hallfred rode to Hreda-water, in North-water dale, where Galti, his brother and a brisk man, managed their matters.

CHAPTER XIII.
Of the Winter-Wedding at Skaney, and how Gunnlaug gave the Kings Cloak to Helga.

Tells the tale of Raven, that he sat at his weddings-feast at Burg, and it was the talk of most men that the bride was but drooping; for true is the saw that saith, "Long we remember what youth gained us," and even so it was with her now.

But this new thing befell at the feast, that Hungerd, the daughter of Thorod and Jofrid, was wooed by a man named Sverting, the son of Hafr-Biorn, the son of Mold-Gnup, and the wedding was to come off that winter after Yule, at Skaney, where dwelt Thorkel, a kinsman of Hungerd, and son of Torn Valbrandsson; and the mother of Torn was Thorodda, the sister of Odd of the Tongue.

Now Raven went home to Mossfell with Helga his wife. When they had been there a little while, one morning early before they rose up, Helga was awake, but Raven slept, and fared ill in his sleep. And when he woke Helga asked him what he had dreamt. Then Raven sang:—

> *"In thine arms, so dreamed I,*
> *Hewn was I, gold island!*
> *Bride, in blood I bled there,*
> *Bed of thine was reddened.*
> *Never more then mightst thou,*
> *Mead-bowl'spourer speedy,*
> *Bind my gashes bloody—*
> *Lind-leek-bough thou likst it."*

Helga spake: "Never shall I weep therefor," quoth she; "ye have evilly beguiled me, and Gunnlaug has surely come out." And therewith she wept much.

But, a little after, Gunnlaug's coming was bruited about, and Helga became so hard with Raven, that he could not keep her at home at Mossfell; so that back they had to go to Burg, and Raven got small share of her company.

Now men get ready for the winter-wedding. Thorkel of Skaney bade Illugi the Black and his sons. But when master Illugi got ready, Gunnlaug sat in the hall, and stirred not to go. Illugi went up to him and said, "Why dost thou not get ready, kinsman?"

Gunnlaug answered, "I have no mind to go."

Says Illugi, "Nay, but certes thou shalt go, kinsman," says he; "and cast thou not grief over thee by yearning for one woman. Make as if thou knewest nought of it, for women thou wilt never lack."

Now Gunnlaug did as his father bade him; so they came to the wedding, and Illugi and his sons were set down in the high seat; but Thorstein Egilson, and Raven his son-in-law, and the bridegroom's following, were set in the other high seat, over against Illugi.

The women sat on the dais, and Helga the Fair sat next to the bride. Oft she turned her eyes on Gunnlaug, thereby proving the saw, "Eyes will bewray if maid love man."

Gunnlaug was well arrayed, and had on him that goodly raiment that King Sigtrygg had given him; and now he was thought far above all other men, because of many things, both strength, and goodliness, and growth.

There was little mirth among folk at this wedding. But on the day when all men were making ready to go away the women stood up and got ready to go home. Then went Gunnlaug to talk to Helga, and long they talked together: but Gunnlaug sang:—

> *"Light-heart lived the Worm-tongue*
> *All day long no longer*
> *In mountain-home, since Helga*
> *Had name of wife of Raven;*
> *Nought foresaw thy father,*
> *Hardener white of fight-thaw,*
> *What my words should come to.*
> *—The maid to gold was wedded."*

And again he sang:—

> *"Worst reward I owe them,*
> *Father thine, O wine-may,*

> *And mother, that they made thee*
> *So fair beneath thy maid-gear;*
> *For thou, sweet field of sea-flame,*
> *All joy hast slain within me.—*
> *Lo, here, take it, loveliest*
> *E'er made of lord and lady!"*

And therewith Gunnlaug gave Helga the cloak, Ethelred's-gift, which was the fairest of things, and she thanked him well for the gift.

Then Gunnlaug went out, and by that time riding-horses had been brought home and saddled, and among them were many very good ones; and they were all tied up in the road. Gunnlaug leaps on to a horse, and rides a hand-gallop along the homefield up to a place where Raven happened to stand just before him; and Raven had to draw out of his way. Then Gunnlaug said,—

"No need to slink aback, Raven, for I threaten thee nought as at this time; but thou knowest forsooth, what thou hast earned.".

Raven answered and sang,—

> *"God of wound-flamed glitter,*
> *Glorier of fight-goddess,*
> *Must we fall a-fighting*
> *For fairest kirtle-bearer?*
> *Death-staffs many such-like*
> *Fair as she is are there*
> *In south-lands o'er the sea floods.*
> *Sooth saith he who knoweth."*

"Maybe there are many such, but they do not seem so to me," said Gunnlaug.

Therewith Illugi and Thorstein ran up to them, and would not have them fight.

Then Gunnlaug sang,—

"The fair-hued golden goddess
For gold to Raven sold they,
(Raven my match as men say)
While the mighty isle-king,
Ethelred, in England
From eastward way delayed me,
Wherefore to gold-waster
Waneth tongue's speech-hunger."

Hereafter both rode home, and all was quiet and tidingless that winter through; but Raven had nought of Helga's fellowship after her meeting with Gunnlaug.

CHAPTER XIV.
Of the Holmgang at the Althing.

Now in summer men ride a very many to the Althing: Illugi the Black and his sons with him, Gunnlaug and Hermund; Thorstein Egilson and Kolsvein his son; Onund, of Mossfell, and his sons all, and Sverting, Hafr-Biorn's son. Skapti yet held the spokesmanship-at-law.

One day at the Thing, as men went thronging to the Hill of Laws, and when the matters of the law were done there, then Gunnlaug craved silence, and said:—

"Is Raven, the son of Onund, here?"

He said he was.

Then spake Gunnlaug, "Thou well knowest that thou hast got to wife my avowed bride, and thus hast thou made thyself my foe. Now for this I bid thee to holm here at the Thing, in the holm of the Axe-water, when three nights are gone by."

Raven answers, "This is well bidden, as was to be looked for of thee, and for this I am ready, whenever thou wiliest it."

Now the kin of each deemed this a very ill thing. But, at that time it was lawful for him who thought himself wronged by another to call him to fight on the holm.

So when three nights had gone by they got ready for the holmgang, and Illugi the Black followed his son thither with a great following. But Skapti, the lawman, followed Raven, and his father and other kinsmen of his.

Now before Gunnlaug went upon the holm he sang,—

> *"Out to isle ofeel-field*
>
> *Dight am I to hie me:*
>
> *Give, O God, thy singer*
>
> *With glaive to end the striving.*
>
> *Here shall I the head cleave*
>
> *Of Helga's love's devourer,*
>
> *At last my bright sword bringeth*
>
> *Sundering of head and body."*

Then Raven answered and sang,—

> *"Thou, singer, knowest not surely*
> *Which of us twain shall gain it;*
> *With edge for leg-swathe eager,*
> *Here are the wound-scythes bare now.*
> *In whatso-wise we wound us,*
> *The tidings from the Thing here,*
> *And fame of thanes' fair doings,*
> *The fair young maid shall hear it."*

Hermund held shield for his brother, Gunnlaug; but Sverting, Hafr-Biorn's son, was Raven's shield-bearer. Whoso should be wounded was to ransom himself from the holm with three marks of silver.

Now, Raven's part it was to deal the first blow, as he was the challenged man. He hewed at the upper part of Gunnlaug's shield, and the sword brake asunder just beneath the hilt, with so great might he smote; but the point of the sword flew up from the shield and struck Gunnlaug's cheek, whereby he got just grazed; with that their fathers ran in between them, and many other men.

"Now," said Gunnlaug, "I call Raven overcome, as he is weaponless."

"But I say that thou art vanquished, since thou art wounded," said Raven.

Now, Gunnlaug was nigh mad, and very wrathful, and said it was not tried out yet.

Illugi, his father, said they should try no more for that time.

Gunnlaug said, "Beyond all things I desire that I might in such wise meet Raven again, that thou, father, wert not anigh to part us."

And thereat they parted for that time, and all men went back to their booths.

But on the second day after this it was made law in the law-court that, henceforth, all holmgangs should be forbidden; and this was done by the counsel of all the wisest men that were at the Thing; and there, indeed, were all the men of most counsel in all the land. And this was the last holmgang fought in Iceland, this, wherein Gunnlaug and Raven fought.

But this Thing was the third most thronged Thing that has been held in Iceland; the first was after Njal's burning, the second after the Heath-slaughters.

Now, one morning, as the brothers Hermund and Gunnlaug went to Axe-water to wash, on the other side went many women towards the river, and in that company was Helga the Fair. Then said Hermund,—

"Dost thou see thy friend Helga there on the other side of the river?"

"Surely, I see her," says Gunnlaug, and withal he sang:—

> *"Born was she for men's bickering:*
> *Sore bale hath wrought the war-stemy*
> *And I yearned ever madly*
> *To hold that oak-tree golden.*
> *To me then, me destroyer*
> *Of swan-mead's flame, unneedful*
> *This looking on the dark-eyed,*
> *This golden land's beholding."*

Therewith they crossed the river, and Helga and Gunnlaug spake awhile together, and as the brothers crossed the river eastward back again, Helga stood and gazed long after Gunnlaug.

Then Gunnlaug looked back and sang:—

> *"Moon of linen-lapped one,*
> *Leek-sea-bearing goddess,*
> *Hawk-keen out of heaven*
> *Shone all bright upon me;*
> *But that eyelid's moonbeam*
> *Of gold-necklaced goddess*
> *Her hath all undoing*
> *Wrought, and me made nought of."*

CHAPTER XV.
How Gunnlaug and Raven agreed to go East to Norway, to try the matter again.

Now after these things were gone by men rode home from the Thing, and Gunnlaug dwelt at home at Gilsbank.

On a morning when he awoke all men had risen up, but he alone still lay abed; he lay in a shut-bed behind the seats. Now into the hall came twelve men, all full armed, and who should be there but Raven, Onund's son; Gunnlaug sprang up forthwith, and got to his weapons.

But Raven spake, "Thou art in risk of no hurt this time," quoth he, "but my errand hither is what thou shalt now hear: Thou didst call me to a holmgang last summer at the Althing, and thou didst not deem matters to be fairly tried therein; now I will offer thee this, that we both fare away from Iceland, and go abroad next summer, and go on holm in Norway, for there our kinsmen are not like to stand in our way."

Gunnlaug answered, "Hail to thy words, stoutest of men! this thine offer I take gladly; and here, Raven, mayest thou have cheer as good as thou mayest desire."

"It is well offered," said Raven, "but this time we shall first have to ride away." Thereon they parted.

Now the kinsmen of both sore misliked them of this, but could in no wise undo it, because of the wrath of Gunnlaug and Raven; and, after all, that must betide that drew towards.

Now it is to be said of Raven that he fitted out his ship in Leiruvag; two men are named that went with him, sisters' sons of his father Onund, one hight Grim, the other Olaf, doughty men both. All the kinsmen of Raven thought it great scathe when he went away, but he said he had challenged Gunnlaug to the holmgang because he could have no joy soever of Helga; and he said, withal, that one must fall before the other.

So Raven put to sea, when he had wind at will, and brought his ship to Thrandheim, and was there that winter and heard nought of Gunnlaug that winter through; there lie abode him the summer following: and still another winter was he in Thrandheim, at a place called Lifangr.

Gunnlaug Worm-tongue took ship with Hallfred Troublous-Skald, in the north at The Plain; they were very late ready for sea.

They sailed into the main when they had a fair wind, and made Orkney a little before the winter. Earl Sigurd Lodverson was still lord over the isles, and Gunnlaug went to him and abode there that winter, and the earl held him of much account.

In the spring the earl would go on warfare, and Gunnlaug made ready to go with him; and that summer they harried wide about the South-isles and Scotland's firths, and had many fights, and Gunnlaug always showed himself the bravest and doughtiest of fellows, and the hardiest of men wherever they came.

Earl Sigurd went back home early in the summer, but Gunnlaug took ship with chapmen, sailing for Norway, and he and Earl Sigurd parted in great friendship.

Gunnlaug fared north to Thrandheim, to Hladir, to see Earl Eric, and dwelt there through the early winter; the earl welcomed him gladly, and made offer to Gunnlaug to stay with him, and Gunnlaug agreed thereto.

The earl had heard already how all had befallen between Gunnlaug and Raven, and he told Gunnlaug that he laid ban on their fighting within his realm; Gunnlaug said the earl should be free to have his will herein.

So Gunnlaug abode there the winter through, ever heavy of mood.

CHAPTER XVI.
How the two Foes met and fought at Dingness.

But on a day in spring Gunnlaug was walking abroad, and his kinsman Thorkel with him; they walked away from the town, till on the meads. before them they saw a ring of men, and in that ring were two men with weapons fencing; but one was named Raven, the other Gunnlaug, while they who stood by said that Icelanders smote light, and were slow to remember their words.

Gunnlaug saw the great mocking hereunder, and much jeering was brought into the play; and withal he went away silent.

So a little while after he said to the earl that he had no mind to bear any longer the jeers and mocks of his courtiers about his dealings with Raven, and therewith he prayed the earl to give him a guide to Lifangr: now before this the earl had been told that Raven had left Lifangr and gone east to Sweden; therefore, he granted Gunnlaug leave to go, and gave him two guides for the journey.

Now Gunnlaug went from Hladir with six men to Lifangr; and, on the morning of the very day whereas Gunnlaug came in in the evening, Raven had left Lifangr with four men. Thence Gunnlaug went to Vera-dale, and came always in the evening to where Raven had been the night before.

So Gunnlaug went on till he came to the uppermost farm in the valley, called Sula, wherefrom had Raven fared in the morning; there he stayed not his journey, but kept on his way through the night.

Then in the morning at sun-rise they saw one another. Raven had got to a place where were two waters, and between them flat meads, and they are called Gleipni's meads: but into one water stretched a little ness called Dingness. There on the ness Raven and his fellows, five together, took their stand. With Raven were his kinsmen, Grim and Olaf.

Now when they met, Gunnlaug said, "It is well that we have found one another."

Raven said that he had nought to quarrel with therein;

"But now," says he, "thou mayest choose as thou wilt, either that we fight alone together, or that we fight all of us man to man."

Gunnlaug said that either way seemed good to him.

Then spake Raven's kinsmen, Grim and Olaf, and said that they would little like to stand by and look on the fight, and in like wise spake Thorkel the Black, the kinsman of Gunnlaug.

Then said Gunnlaug to the earl's guides, "Ye shall sit by and aid neither side, and be here to tell of our meeting;" and so they did.

So they set on, and fought dauntlessly, all of them. Grim and Olaf went both against Gunnlaug alone, and so closed their dealings with him that Gunnlaug slew them both and got no wound. This proves Thord Kolbeinson in a song that he made on Gunnlaug the Wormtongue:—

> *"Grim and Olaf great-hearts*
>
> *In Gondul's din, with thin sword*
>
> *First did Gunnlaug fell there*
>
> *Ere at Raven fared he;*
>
> *Bold, with blood be-drifted*
>
> *Bane of three the thane was;*
>
> *War-lord of the wave-horse*
>
> *Wrought for men folks' slaughter."*

Meanwhile Raven and Thorkel the Black, Gunnlaug's kinsman, fought until Thorkel fell before Raven and lost his life; and so at last all their fellowship fell. Then they two alone fought together with fierce onsets and mighty strokes, which they dealt each the other, falling on furiously without stop or stay.

Gunnlaug had the sword Ethelred's-gift, and that was the best of weapons. At last Gunnlaug dealt a mighty blow at Raven, and cut his leg from under him; but none the more did Raven fall, but swung round up to a tree-stem, whereat he steadied the stump.

Then said Gunnlaug, "Now thou art no more meet for battle, nor will I fight with thee any longer, a maimed man."

Raven answered: "So it is," said he, "that my lot is now all the worser lot, but it were well with me yet, might I but drink somewhat."

Gunnlaug said, "Bewray me not if I bring thee water in my helm."

"I will not bewray thee," said Raven. Then went Gunnlaug to a brook and fetched water in his helm, and brought it to Raven; but Raven stretched forth his left hand to take it, but with his right hand drave his sword into Gunnlaug's head, and that was a mighty great wound.

Then Gunnlaug said, "Evilly hast thou beguiled me, and done traitorously wherein I trusted thee."

Raven answers, "Thou sayest sooth, but this brought me to it, that I begrudged thee to lie in the bosom of Helga the Fair."

Thereat they fought on, recking of nought; but the end of it was that Gunnlaug overcame Raven, and there Raven lost his life..

Then the earl's guides came forward and bound the head-wound of Gunnlaug, and in meanwhile, he sat and sang:—

"O thou sword-storm stirrer,

Raven, stem of battle

Famous, fared against me

Fiercely in the spear din.

Many a flight of metal

Was borne on me this morning,

By the spear-walls' builder,

Ring-bearer, on hard Dingness."

After that they buried the dead, and got Gunnlaug on to his horse thereafter, and brought him right down to Lifangr. There he lay three nights, and got all his rights of a priest, and died thereafter, and was buried at the church there.

All men thought it great scathe of both of these men, Gunnlaug and Raven, amid such deeds as they died.

CHAPTER XVII.
The News of the Fight brought to Iceland.

Now this summer, before these tidings were brought out hither to Iceland, Illugi the Black, being at home at Gilsbank, dreamed a dream: he thought that Gunnlaug came to him in his sleep, all bloody, and he sang in the dream this stave before him; and Illugi remembered the song when he woke, and sang it before others:—

> *"Knew I of the hewing*
> *Of Raven's hilt-finned steel-fish*
> *Byrny-shearing—sword-edge*
> *Sharp clave leg of Raven.—*
> *Of warm wounds drank the eagle,*
> *When the war-rod slender,*
> *Cleaver of the corpses,*
> *Clave the head of Gunnlaug."*

This portent befel south at Mossfell, the self-same night, that Onund dreamed how Raven came to him, covered all over with blood, and sang:—

> *"Red is the sword, but I now*
> *Am undone by Sword-Odin.*
> *'Gainst shields beyond the sea-flood*
> *The ruin of shields was wielded.*
> *Methinks the blood-fowl blood-stained*
> *In blood o'er men's heads stood there,*
> *The wound-erne yet wound-eager*
> *Trod over wounded bodies?"*

Now the second summer after this, Illugi the Black spoke at the Althing from the Hill of Laws, and said:—

"Wherewith wilt thou make atonement to me for my son, whom Raven, thy son, beguiled in his troth?"

Onund answers, "Be it far from me to atone for him, so sorely as their meeting hath wounded me. Yet will I not ask atonement of thee for my son."

"Then shall my wrath come home to some of thy kin," says Illugi. And withal after the Thing was Illugi at most times very sad.

Tells the tale how this autumn Illugi rode from Gilsbank with thirty men, and came to Mossfell early in the morning. Then Onund got into the church with his sons, and took sanctuary; but Illugi caught two of his kin, one called Biorn and the other Thorgrim, and had Biorn slain, but the feet smitten from Thorgrim. And thereafter Illugi rode home, and there was no righting of this for Onund.

Hermund, Illugi's son, had little joy after the death of Gunnlaug his brother, and deemed he was none the more avenged even though this had been wrought.

Now there was a man called Raven, brother's son to Onund of Mossfell; he was a great sea-farer, and had a ship that lay up in Ramfirth: and in the spring Hermund Illugison rode from home alone north over Holt-beacon Heath, even to Ramfirth, and out as far as Board-ere to the ship of the chapmen. The chapmen were then nearly ready for sea; Raven, the ship-master, was on shore, and many men with him; Hermund rode up to him, and thrust him through with his spear, and rode away forthwith: but all Raven's men were bewildered at seeing Hermund.

No atonement came for this slaying, and therewith ended the dealings of Illugi the Black and Onund of Mossfell.

CHAPTER XVIII.
The Death of Helga the Fair.

AS time went on, Thorstein Egilson married his daughter Helga to a man called Thorkel, son of Hallkel, who lived west in Hraundale. Helga went to his house with him, but loved him little, for she cannot cease to think of Gunnlaug, though he be dead. Yet was Thorkel a doughty man, and wealthy of goods, and a good skald.

They had children together not a few, one of them was called Thorarin, another Thorstein, and yet more they had.

But Helga's chief joy was to pluck at the threads of that cloak, Gunnlaug's gift, and she would be ever gazing at it.

But on a time there came a great sickness to the house of Thorkel and Helga, and many were bed-ridden for a long time. Helga also fell sick, and yet she could not keep abed.

So one Saturday evening Helga sat in the fire-hall, and leaned her head upon her husband's knees, and had the cloak Gunnlaug's gift sent for; and when the cloak came to her she sat up and plucked at it, and gazed thereon awhile, and then sank back upon her husband's bosom, and was dead. Then Thorkel sang this:—

> *"Dead in mine arms she droopeth,*
>
> *My dear one, gold-rings bearer,*
>
> *For God hath changed the life-days*
>
> *Of this Lady of the linen.*
>
> *Weary pain hath pined her,*
>
> *But unto me, the seeker*
>
> *Of hoard of fishes highway,*
>
> *Abiding here is wearier."*

Helga was buried in the church there, but Thorkel dwelt yet at Hraundale: but a great matter seemed the death of Helga to all, as was to be looked for.

AND HERE ENDETH THE STORY.

Milton Keynes UK
Ingram Content Group UK Ltd.
UKHW020825231024
450026UK00004B/401